Easter

Program Builder

No. 27

LILLENAS® DRAMA

Easter Program Builder No. 27

Compiled by Kimberly R. Messer

lillenas
PUBLISHING COMPANY

lillenas.com

Questions? Please write or call:
Lillenas Publishing Company
Drama Resources
P.O. Box 419527
Kansas City, MO 64141
Phone: 816-931-1900 • Fax: 816-412-8390
E-mail: drama@lillenas.com
Web Site: www.lillenasdrama.com

Cover Design: Ted Ferguson

Contents

Recitations for Preschool

Happy Easter Day

I'm too little to write down all the
things I want to do and say.
So, Mom had to remind me to come
wish you Happy Easter Day.
Have a Happy Easter Day!

Libby Malloy-Kisseih

Happy, Happy Easter Day

Happy, happy Easter day.
We're oh so glad you came our way
To celebrate God's risen Son.
Please join us as we have some fun!

K. R. Messer

Jesus Carried the Cross

CHILD 1: Jesus carried the cross.
He carried my sins.
He is my Savior.
He is my friend!
CHILD 2: He is God's Son
And I love Him so,
On this Easter Day,
I wanted you to know!

Evangeline Carey

Why We Celebrate

Jesus arose on Easter.
That's why we celebrate.
He came from heaven to earth
To teach us love, not hate.

Stacey A. Schnarr

Shout Hip, Hip Hooray!

(At the end of this piece, have children hold signs to help prompt the congregation to say, "Hip, hip hooray!" Repeat if necessary to get everyone to join in.)

Welcome, welcome to our church
On this happy day.
Welcome, welcome to our church.
Shout, "hip, hip hooray!"
"Hip, hip hooray!"

K. R. Messer

Easter Time

Easter time! Easter time!
Let us say it loud and clear.

Let us sing, shout, and pray.
Jesus Christ is alive today.

Libby Malloy-Kisseih

It's Easter Time!

Oh yeah, oh yeah
It's Easter time!
Let's celebrate God's love.
Oh yeah, oh yeah
It's Easter now.
Jesus came from above.

Oh yeah, oh yeah
It's Easter time.
Christ rose from the dead.
Oh yeah, oh yeah
It's Easter now.
By Him we all are led.

K. R. Messer

Christ is Risen!

CHILD 1: Did you know Christ is risen?
CHILD 2: Yes. He is risen indeed!

Karen Lee

For Communion

I take the bread
I take the cup
At God's feast of love.

I eat the bread
I drink the cup
A sacrifice from above.

K. R. Messer

He Has Risen

CHILD 1: I love Jesus.
I love to call His sweet name.
CHILD 2: I love Jesus.
Everyday He's the same.
CHILD 3: I love Jesus.
My Lord is never far away.
CHILD 4: I love Jesus.
He arose one Easter Day.

Libby Malloy-Kisseih

He's Alive!

He's alive! He's alive!
Praise God today.
He's alive! He's alive!
The stone's been rolled away.

K. R. Messer

If I Were . . .

CHILD 1: If I were a flower,
I would bloom in the spring.
If I were a door bell,
I would go ding-a-ling.
CHILD 2: If I were the sun,
I would shine in the sky.
If I were a bird,
I would know how to fly.
CHILD 3: If I were a bumble bee,
I would make plenty of honey.
If I were the IRS,
I would have to take your money.
CHILD 4: If I were the moon,
I would come out at night.
If I were a star,
I would shine so bright.
CHILD 5: If I were the church pews,
There's one thing I would say.
Jump, sing, and shout,
Don't you know it is Easter Day?

Libby Malloy-Kisseih

Easter's Here

(After the line, "Time to jump for joy," have one or two children hop across the stage or have the group reciting jump a few times.)

Easter, Easter, Easter's here!
Time to jump for joy!
Easter, Easter, Easter's here
For every girl and boy.

K. R. Messer

Recitations for Ages 5 to 7

Believe the Good News This Easter!

CHILD 1: Believe the Good News
this Easter.
Jesus is no longer in the
grave!
He got up, up, up!
An angel rolled the stone
away!
CHILD 2: He arose! He arose!
His death and burial is
done!
He went back to heaven
To prepare us a brand-new
home!

Evangeline Carey

He Loves Us So

I got this new dress for Easter
And I'm sure it fits me well.
But I am not one for bragging,
I am sure this you can tell.

Now that I have your attention,
There's one thing I want you to
know.
Jesus died and arose on Easter Day,
Because He loves us so.

Libby Malloy-Kisseih

Proclaim It!

Today we proclaim it,
That wonderful, glorious theme.
Alleluia! He is risen!
Christ is risen indeed!

Karen Lee

E-A-S-T-E-R

E is for *everything* Jesus means to
me.
A is for *always* a friend He will be.
S is for He's a *special* person in my
life.
T is for He *takes* away the heartache
and strife.
E is for Jesus' *endless* love He shows
in every way.
R is for *remembering* Jesus arose on
Easter Day.

Libby Mallow-Kisseih

I Won't Let Go of Jesus!

I won't let go of Jesus!
I won't let go of God!
I have made a special place
For Jesus in my heart!

I have hope in Him,
I have peace too.
If you'll accept Him as Savior,
There'll be hope and peace for you!

Evangeline Carey

Let Him in Your Heart

Today you've heard the story
Of the sacrifice Jesus made.
We hope you'll let Him in your
heart
And give Him a place to stay.

K. R. Messer

I Want You to Know

Yes, I know you have noticed this
  Fine Easter suit I have on.
But, have you seen my new shining
  Shoes or smelled my sweet
    cologne?

Now that I've got your attention,
  There's one thing I want to say.
I hope you have a spirit-filled
  And beautiful Easter Day.

Libby Malloy-Kesseih

Spend Time With Jesus This Easter Day!

Spend time with Jesus
This Easter Day.
Be thankful to Him
As you pray!

He gave so much
To set us free,
Bringing hope and peace
And life eternally!

Evangeline Carey

Rejoice!

Easter morning dawns,
A beautiful sunny day.
Christ our Lord has risen,
Our ransom He did pay.

Rejoice in His resurrection.
He sits upon the throne.
Praise His name forever.
Eternal life—our own.

Karen Lee

New Life

Easter comes at springtime,
A beautiful time of year
When the earth is full of new life
And hearts begin to cheer.

Easter brought us new life
When Christ defeated death.
Let's celebrate eternal life
With every single breath.

Karen Lee

Spring is Everywhere

Spring is everywhere you look.
It's green as green can be.
Today we celebrate Easter day
And God's love for you and me.

K. R. Messer

The Joyful Sound

Easter bells are ringing
Here and all around.
Listen to the clanging
Of the joyful sound.

Christ our Lord is risen
From the dark domain.
We lift on high His praises,
And bless His holy name.

Robert Colbert

This Easter Day, Worship Heaven's King!

This Easter Day
Worship Heaven's King.
Share in the hope
And salvation He brings!

Evangeline Carey

True Joy

It's Easter morn
True joy is born.
Happy resurrection
To everyone!

Robert Colbert

Easter Joy

It was so sad on Friday
To see the Savior die,
To feel the pain of loss
And for a friend to cry.

But what a joyful morning
This Easter day becomes
Because my Savior lives,
And my Friend—for life—has won!

Karen Lee

He Washed All Our Sins Away

(Encourage each CHILD *to act out each verse or draw and paint pictures on poster board for the congregation to see.)*

CHILD 1: I know why the birds sing
Such a sweet melody.
It's because God taught
Them never to sing off-key.

CHILD 2: I know why the snow is so white
As it slowly falls from on high.
It's because God washes His hands
Before He throws it from the sky.

CHILD 3: I know why the grass looks like a beautiful
Green blanket that covers the ground.
It is because our God wants us to have a
Nice place to put our feet down.

CHILD 4: I know why we are celebrating
This bright Easter Day.
It's because when Jesus died,
He washed all our sins away.

Libby Malloy-Kisseih

Recitations for Ages 8 to 10

Easter Cheer

(This "cheer" should be led by an older child or a group of children for the congregation or a children's service. Use posters that are easy to read to help prompt the audience to do their part—E-A-S-T-E-R. You can also create different formations to the natural rhythm of the piece with the kids such as a cheering squad might do. Immediately follow up the cheer with an upbeat song.)

E-A-S-T-E-R
Say "E-A-S-T-E-R"
(Repeat)
Easter is a time for us
To celebrate God's love.
He sent His one and only Son
To earth from heaven above.
Today we welcome all of you
And hope you'll join the fun.

E-A-S-T-E-R
Say "E-A-S-T-E-R"
(Repeat)
Happy Easter!

K. R. Messer

What Would I Have Done?

If I had been Mary
That morning so drear,
Would I have been brave
Or been hiding in fear?

Would I have taken
The perfume to Him
Or stayed home, pretending
The day wasn't grim?

I would have joined Mary,
Trusting God above,
And I would have heard
My name called with love.

I, too, would have run
To proclaim in accord,
Christ is risen! He is risen!
I've seen the Lord!

Karen Lee

What Jesus Can Do

Welcome to *(insert name of church)*!
We're glad you came to celebrate
Easter Day with us.
Today you'll learn Jesus' fate.
Listen up, you must.

We saw our Savior on the cross.
Misery and pain.
But he was dying for the lost.
Precious souls to gain.

On the third day he rose again.
Con'qring death and sin.
His blood has cleansed the hearts of men.
Makes us pure within.

Give your life to Jesus today.
He will fill your heart
With perfect peace in every way.
He's the missing part.

Stacey A. Schnarr

Blessings

Blessings on Easter
For all I pray,
Jesus has risen
And is here to stay.

Jesus has risen!
To all I shout,
He walks among us
That never doubt.

Christopher J. Todd

He Is Risen

"Christ is risen
There's nothing to fear!"
The angel proclaimed
For disciples to hear.

He's done what He promised,
He conquered the grave!
Descending from heaven,
His mission: to save.

His mercy is endless
Soft eyes, full of love.
His blood made us holy,
As white as a dove.

So lift up your voices,
Our Father be praised!
Proclaim of His glory,
Our Jesus is raised!

Jessica Andres

Plays, Sketches & Monologues for All Ages

Easter

by Martha S. Campbell

Creative Presentation Idea: The poem, "Easter," could be used by juniors or youth as a pantomime. This could be for a sunrise service or for other Easter worship.

Cast:

READER
MARY—dressed in light, flowing robe
JOHN—dressed in a dark or striped robe, with headdress
PETER—same as John
ANGELS or ANGEL VOICE—offstage voice(s)
JESUS—dressed in a white or light robe; a deep voice is suggested

Early, very early, before the day was born
Mary went into the garden, her dear Lord to mourn
Because her dear friend, Jesus, had been buried there.
Her heart was very heavy, almost more than she could bear.

When she reached the garden, she was indeed surprised;
The tomb was very empty; she couldn't believe her eyes!
Away to John and Peter on her swift feet she sped,
"They've taken away my Lord," she breathlessly said.
They ran back together, hoping to see Jesus' face;
But only linen cloths were a-lying in the place.
Back home the disciples went, for they did not know
That Jesus had arisen, as He had told them. So,

Mary stayed in the garden and, as daylight began,
She wept and she cried; oh, how the tears ran!
She looked in the tomb, saw two angels inside;
They asked, "Why are you crying?" to which she replied;

"I don't know where they have taken my Lord,"
then she turned, saw a Man pierced with a sword
Who asked, "Why are you crying? Whom do you seek?"
Mary answered, "For Jesus, my Lord; I want just a peek."

The Man, who was Jesus, spoke, "Mary," He said;
The voice! It was Jesus! She had nothing to dread.
He was alive, in the garden; He talked to her more,
"Go tell the others, but don't touch me," He implored.

Away ran Mary on that first Easter morn;
"Jesus is alive. No more will we mourn!
We talked in the garden; I've seen Him," she said.
The disciples were happy; Jesus had risen from the dead!

And so, we too can be happy; sing al-le-lu-ia!
The message is clear; sing al-le-lu-ia!
We too can live again, just only believe.
He calls us by name, and us will receive!

(For closing, the congregation or choir may sing "Christ the Lord Is Risen Today" by Charles Wesley.)

The Favor of God

by Sara Ann Denson

Cast:

YOUNG MARY—a young girl
PAPA—a strong man with a beard
TEENAGE MARY—a young woman carrying a basket
ANGEL—offstage voice
OLDER MARY—a woman wearing robes splattered with bloodlike substance; face is uncovered
THREE WOMEN—two younger, one older; robes also splattered with bloodlike substance; faces may be covered
JOHN—young disciple of Jesus, clothes blood splattered, face uncovered
SOLDIER 1—offstage voice
SOLDIER 2—offstage voice
CHRIST—offstage voice

Summary: Mary was a young Jewish woman who was raised on the stories of her ancestors, stories that taught her to respect and obey God. Her life represents so many of us who are in Christian service, who gladly answer the call as young people, but then face pain in the ministry and still must obey the will of God. The phases of Mary's life, represented back and forth in this play, show how interconnected her obedience was throughout the course of her history; waiting for the Messiah as a Jew, receiving the Messiah as a mother, accepting the Messiah's payment for sin as a human being.

Setting: Three stage areas are set up, even if they are only divided by lighting. One stage area is set to the right, one center, one left. On the first stage is where the Young Mary and Papa walk across. The second area is where the Teenaged Mary receives the news that she is to bear the Messiah. The third area is where the Older Mary wrestles with God over the fate of her son on the cross.

Scene 1

(YOUNG MARY *enters on stage one with* PAPA.)

YOUNG MARY *(holding hands with* PAPA, *swinging his hand and pulling him along):* Papa, tell me again about Enoch.

PAPA: Mary, I've told you three times already.

YOUNG MARY: But Papa, I love that story! I love how God takes him away to heaven. *(Sweeps up her hands as* PAPA *laughs and swings her around.)*

PAPA: Ah, my dear one, we have awhile yet before we are home again. Enoch was a man who lived long ago when very few people loved God. He talked to God every day and found favor in God's eyes. When the time came, he didn't die like your grandmother or your Uncle Josiah. God came and took him to heaven.

YOUNG MARY: Will the Messiah go to God that way?

PAPA: The Messiah? Ha! The Messiah—He will never die. He will live forever. He will be different than all; like Noah, He will survive all that will happen. But Noah eventually died. The Messiah—He will never, ever die!

YOUNG MARY: Tell me about Noah, Papa. *(They exit.)*

Scene 2

(On second/middle stage, TEENAGE MARY *enters with large basket, gathering kindling for a fire.)*

ANGEL: Greetings, you who are highly favored! The Lord is with you.

*(*TEENAGE MARY *drops basket, spins around to see who is there; stops, facing the audience. A light hits her face. She squints painfully, shields her face and falls backward. Freezes with light still on her.)*

Scene 3

*(*YOUNG MARY *and* PAPA *enter on stage one; walking across stage area.)*

YOUNG MARY: But why did God save Noah, Papa, and not all those other people?

PAPA: Sweet child, why so many questions today?

YOUNG MARY: I want to know all about our fathers who loved God. How did God know they loved Him?

PAPA: He knew because they talked to Him. They prayed and when they heard His voice, they listened and obeyed.

YOUNG MARY: Were they different, Papa? Were they stronger and more powerful? Is that why God talked to them?

PAPA: No, Mary, they were normal people. They started out as babies like your sister. You were a baby once. Just as we all were. (They exit.)

Scene 4

(On middle stage, TEENAGE MARY *is still frozen under the light.)*

ANGEL: Do not be afraid, Mary, you have found favor with God. *(MARY slowly lowers arm so that her face is seen.)* You will be with child *(touches abdomen and bows head, slowly looking up to listen)*, and give birth to a Son, and you are to give Him the name Jesus. He will be great and will be called the Son of the Most High. *(MARY looks back and forth as if to solve a mystery; mouths the word "Messiah" as she figures it out, becoming excited.)* The Lord God will give Him the throne of His father David, and He will reign over the house of Jacob forever; His kingdom will never end.

TEENAGE MARY *(overjoyed, but wanting details)*: How will this be since I am a virgin?

ANGEL: The Holy Spirit will come upon you, and the power of the Most High will overshadow you. So the Holy One to be born will be called the Son of God. Even Elizabeth, your relative, is going to have a child in her old age, and she who was said to be barren is in her sixth month. For nothing is impossible with God.

(MARY freezes again with a look of wonder and praise, youthful courage and faith.)

Scene 5

(On third stage, OLDER MARY enters with THREE WOMEN and JOHN. They stand huddled together, watching in horror and disbelief as they listen to the SOLDIERS' voices. They are looking both to their left where the SOLDIERS supposedly are, and above where CHRIST hangs on the cross. Neither CHRIST nor the SOLDIERS are actually onstage. Main focus is on OLDER MARY and her reaction to the moment at the foot of the cross when her world falls apart.)

SOLDIER 1 *(mocking)*: The robe of the Messiah. Anybody want a piece of this?

SOLDIER 2: Wait! Let's not tear it. Let's decide by lot who will get it.

(SFX: rustling and swords clattering; CHRIST groans.)

MARY *(in shock, speaking to WOMEN hovering around her)*: The garment is seamless like the high priests wear. I wove it for Him and prayed over it for His protection; that Yahweh would raise Him up to free us all. He is the Messiah. The Messiah. The Messiah of all people should be swept up into the clouds as Elijah.

JOHN *(calming her)*: He is the Messiah. Even now the scriptures are fulfilled: "They divided my garments . . ."

MARY/JOHN *(MARY looking at JOHN in shock, but holding onto words)*: "among them and cast lots for my clothing." *(MARY tries to calm herself to God's will. They freeze.)*

Scene 6

*(*YOUNG MARY *and* PAPA *enter on stage one.* MARY *skips beside* PAPA, *pretending to pick flowers.)*

YOUNG MARY: Papa, Abraham and Moses found favor with God. He fulfilled His promises to them too. Someday, God will find favor on us and will send us the Messiah. I would be a warrior if He asked me. *(Picks up stick and swings it like a sword.)*

PAPA: A warrior, my dear child? Better to let your brothers learn to fight. You can serve God by learning to sew and pray.

YOUNG MARY: I will pray, Papa, so that I can see the prophecies fulfilled just as Abraham and Moses. I want to see our people freed.

PAPA *(sighing):* It would be nice to have our people united under a King David as in days of old, but we must remember the lessons of the promises fulfilled in Abraham and Moses. God kept His promises, yes, but the promises were answered differently than they expected and took many, many years. We must only wait and pray and be willing to do whatever He asks.

YOUNG MARY: Papa, when He asks me, I'll be like Samuel. I'll say . . . *(they freeze)*

Scene 7

(Lights up on OLDER MARY *at cross.)*

OLDER MARY: How can this be? *(Looks around panicked and crumples among the* WOMEN.*)* How can His death be a fulfillment of all our hopes for freedom? He is my son. *(Angrily)* My son. How can I give up my son?

CHRIST: Mother?

JOHN: He speaks, Mary. *(Drawing her forward.)*

CHRIST: John?

OLDER MARY: My sweet child . . .

CHRIST *(lovingly, a halting voice):* Dear woman, here is your son. *(To* JOHN.*)* Here is your mother. *(*MARY *cries against* JOHN'S *shoulder.)*

JOHN *(holding* MARY*)*: She will be of my household from now forward. *(They freeze.)*

Scene 8

(Lights on middle stage where TEENAGE MARY *repeats part of former scene.)*

TEENAGE MARY: How will this be since I am a virgin?

ANGEL: The Holy Spirit will come upon you, and the power of the Most High will over shadow you. So the Holy One to be born will be called the Son of God. Even Elizabeth, your relative, is going to have a child in her old age, and she who was said to be barren is in her sixth month. For nothing is impossible with God.

(Lights on all three MARY'S.*)*

YOUNG MARY *(happily):* Papa, I'll shout, "I am the Lord's Servant." *(Light out.)*

TEENAGE MARY *(resolutely, with excitement and passion):* I am the Lord's Servant. May it be to me as you have said. *(Light brightens, then out.)*

OLDER MARY *(struggling into submission):* I am the Lord's Servant. May it be to me as you have said. *(Light out.)*

Saturday

A Reader's Theatre piece for six voices on the day after the Crucifixion

by Robert Shuttleworth

Cast:

PETER—READER 1
JUDAS—READER 2
MARY MAGDALENE—READER 3
MARY THE MOTHER OF JESUS—READER 4
THOMAS—READER 5
PILATE—READER 6

Author's note: The day between Good Friday and Easter Sunday in the Christian calendar (often referred to as Holy Saturday) is an awkward one for most Christians. It is a day of questions, of contemplation, of reassessing their faith. But what of those who were part of the events of that week? How did they feel and what were they thinking? The man they had called, among other things, Teacher and Messiah had just been betrayed and cruelly executed. How was this possible? But were the things He said and the prophecies that proceeded Him true? Could a man so brutally killed actually rise again? These thoughts must have been in their minds on that fateful Saturday. For even those of the greatest faith have questions, and it is through their faith that those questions are answered.

Setting: Stage is set with six stools each with a music stand in front of it. Each music stand has a light on it that can be operated by the performer, this is the primary lighting source for the entire piece. If microphone stands are being used, they should be fixed and adjusted prior to the performance to minimize movement as the actors take their places. These six areas should be scattered throughout the available space, and spread as much as is practical. They should form no recognizable pattern. If platforms are available, utilizing them to place the actors on a number of levels can add to the presentation.

(At appropriate time house lights will come down and READERS *will enter the space in near darkness. When they are seated, there should be a blackout and a brief pause to allow the audience to settle. Just before each* READER *speaks their first line, they will turn on their own stand light.* READERS *should not address or look at each other directly. They are "speaking their thoughts" and the other voices heard are within their own mind as they contemplate the crucifixion of Jesus. It is to these "voices" that each* READER *should react as an actor.)*

PETER: Gone!

JUDAS: Forever.

MARY MAGDALENE: How?

MARY MOTHER OF JESUS: Why?

THOMAS: Unbelievable!

PILATE: Unthinkable.

MARY MAGDALENE: But He said . . .

THOMAS: What He said doesn't matter anymore.

MARY MOTHER OF JESUS: It matters to me.

PILATE: I never thought, never realized . . .

PETER: Where can I go now? I can't . . .

MARY MAGDALENE: We will have to wait.

THOMAS: You can't possibly think that . . .

MARY MOTHER OF JESUS: It doesn't matter what we think. What matters is what He did . . .

MARY MAGDALENE: We have to do what is expected.

JUDAS: I didn't expect this.

PETER: None of us did.

PILATE: I wanted no part of it.

THOMAS: How are we supposed to continue? Where are we supposed to go? What are we supposed to do now?

PETER: We were told weren't we? Didn't we listen? Or was it just that we didn't truly believe?

MARY MAGDALENE: You should have done more. All of you.

PILATE: Leave me out of this. I didn't want to be any part of it.

JUDAS: Neither did I, but here I am, right in the middle . . .

MARY MOTHER OF JESUS: How can you say that. You were the one who . . . who . . .

MARY MAGDALENE: That's right! I saw the whole thing.

PETER: I was there also. But I'm not certain that we are the ones to judge him. I don't think He would have wanted us to.

THOMAS: I doubt that any of us actually had any control over any of it.

PETER: Maybe I'm wrong, but I remember now how He warned us it would happen.

PILATE: It was as if He knew what was coming and still allowed it to happen. *(Beat)* In spite of everything else . . . He could have saved himself . . . couldn't He?

MARY MAGDALENE: Of course He knew, but what does that matter now, there is nothing more He can do for us.

THOMAS: Are you so sure of that? Remember what He said, and what the Scriptures say.

PILATE: That's why there are guards at His tomb. I've heard the rumors, and know what the Scriptures say . . .

JUDAS: You don't really think . . .

PILATE: Don't be absurd. There will be no miracles in the morning. The guards are there to assure that.

PETER: Don't any of you realize what we have lost?

MARY MOTHER OF JESUS: You merely lost a friend . . .

PETER: We have lost our mentor, our leader, our soul . . .

PILATE: Leave me out of it. I never knew Him. He was no friend of mine.

JUDAS: You're still a part of it. A pawn like me.

THOMAS: I don't believe this. He's gone and if it weren't for you, He'd still be here.

PETER: That's not fair . . . and it's not what we've been taught these past few years. We all had our parts in this. But what do we do now?

THOMAS: There is so much that I still don't understand. How will I receive the answers now? Who will give them to me?

MARY MOTHER OF JESUS: What is there to understand? An innocent man is now dead and lies in a tomb.

MARY MAGDALENE: He showed me compassion, as no one else ever had. I would have followed Him forever. *(Pause)* He has no more answers for any of us now. Although . . .

PILATE: He was a man, and now He's dead. Nothing can change that. Be realistic.

JUDAS: You could have prevented it. You had a choice . . .

THOMAS *(sharply):* So did you! *(Calmer)* In fact, so did He. But that's just the question. Could anything have stopped it? He seemed to know what was going to happen. He even predicted it. But He did nothing to stop it. Why?

PETER: You still don't understand, do you? He told us any number of times. We just didn't understand what He was saying until it was too late. I don't think we can blame any one person. I don't think He truly wanted to destroy himself, but He seemed to know that events of the past week were unavoidable. I thought that nothing could shake my faith. But His total lack of resistance to being taken away, even healing that man's injured ear as He was being taken. I think that if He had wanted to, He *could* have saved himself. But He knew that He had a different path to follow.

PILATE: You know, it wasn't until after He was led away that I realized that I had had no control at all over any of the events. *He* was the one who guided them, even when He was silent. I was secure in my position, with few cares. Even after I washed my hands of this Man's fate, attempting to convince myself that I was now separated from it, I knew, deep inside myself, that I had been changed by His mere presence. *(Feigned confidence)* But now, it's over. In a few weeks I'll forget this Man and everything will be normal again . . . won't it?

MARY MAGDALENE: Where can I go now? It seems as if He granted me a new existence. Before He came into my life I was truly lost, not caring about anything except for myself and what was needed to survive another day. Then, through Him, everything changed. But now, without Him, I'm not sure that I can still go on.

MARY MOTHER OF JESUS: You, all of you, lost a friend and teacher. I lost that which had been a part of me.

PETER: He was a part of all of us.

MARY MOTHER OF JESUS: No! . . . I don't care what He was to you, what He said to you, or what you think He may have been. I knew what He was and where He came from long before anyone else. I was the one who carried Him for nine months, and bore Him in a stable. I cared for Him as my husband and I fled to Egypt, and later returned to watch Him grow to manhood. It was I who watched Him as He left His home and sought out new companions and the new life that had been laid out for Him before His birth. Finally, . . . I watched as He suffered and died even as those companions, whom He loved, betrayed and fled from Him. None of you can be that much a part of Him. (Pause) These good women who have followed Him will attend to His earthly body in the morning. I will go with His loved disciple, and mourn Him in my own way.

THOMAS: I was neither the first, nor was I the last to be asked to follow Him. But follow Him I did. I don't know why He allowed me to stay with Him. I was always the one asking questions, always needing some type of proof. But the Man I came to believe in is now gone. What do I believe now? Will I ever have the proof that He is, or was, what we thought Him to be?

JUDAS: I believed too . . . at first . . . but then something began to make me feel that everything was changing. There was no way to control the events that were occurring all around us. People . . . powerful people were angered at us. We were all in danger. I thought I could calm everything down. I didn't realize everything that could happen. I just didn't think. I tried to stop it, but it was beyond my control, even at the beginning. *(Pause)* He seemed to understand that. *(Pause)* But how did He know it would be me, and why was I selected to be the instrument of His destruction? Where do I go from here? How can I live with what I have done? *(Turns off light.)*

PETER: Why did He choose me? I was the first. What was it about Him that made me leave everything that I had known all my life to follow Him, and to listen and to believe? *(Pause)* I remember looking at His eyes that first time He spoke to me. It was as if a hot knife had cut into my heart . . . but it was not painful. It was wonderful, and that heat spread joy throughout my soul. I was powerless to resist His presence. He said, one time, that I would be the foundation of His Church. But I am only a poor fisherman, or at least I was . . . before. *(Pause)* I promised Him that I would always be faithful and never leave His side, but then denied Him as quickly as I had followed Him. But He had told me that it would be so. How did He know, and why did He have to die?

PILATE *(distracted):* This night seems darker than any that I can remember. The whole city must be able to feel it. Particularly after the earthquake. I was informed that it occurred at the moment of His death, and just moments before that He had asked His God to forgive everyone who had done this to Him. Or was He trying to say something more? What do I make of that? *(Pause)* How long will it be until dawn? *(Pause)* There is a rumbling among His followers that He will return from death. I understand that their religious Scriptures even predict it. How can that be? A man doesn't return from death, especially from death on the cross. *(Pause)* Curse this darkness! *(Pause)* There was no doubt from those who took Him down. They all agreed He was dead! *(Pause)* Will it ever be light again? *(Turns off light.)*

MARY MAGDALENE: I told His mother that I would help in tending to Him in the morning, although I don't know if I can go through with it. It's not the idea of the body that worries me. Heaven knows I've seen enough of them in my lifetime . . . both alive and dead. I just don't know if I can stand to see *Him* lying there. There was so much life in Him that He gave a part of it to anyone who ever came near to Him or listened to Him, including myself. *(Pause)* I feel now as if I've lost a part of myself. What will I do after tomorrow morning? *(Turns off light.)*

THOMAS: I doubt I'll ever meet anyone like Him again. Was He who He claimed to be? Will I ever be able to prove it to myself? The men I have come to call brothers are scattered this evening. Where will I find them? Even if I do I doubt if they will have the answers. All the same, we must come together again. But without Him to guide us, how will I continue to believe? *(Turns off light.)*

MARY MOTHER OF JESUS: My son is lost to me now. Others who share my name will go in the morning to prepare Him as is our custom. They would have gone today, but it is the Sabbath and our law forbids it. From His execution site, He asked His friend to care for me, and I know that he will. So I'll go with my new son and remain with him. But where will my life go from here? What will it be, and why couldn't He be here to care for me? I, more than anyone, should be able to understand, but as a mother how can I? After they complete their tasks in the morning . . . where will my life go? *(Turns off light.)*

PETER: I feel so alone tonight, and I don't think I'm the only one. I've followed and believed in a man for so long now, that my previous life is little more than a shadowy memory. My life became so filled with His thoughts and teachings that I could not allow myself to think of a life without Him. Then He was ripped away from me as we, who had been asked to stay with Him, slept. Then I denied even knowing Him as He said I would. But He also said that I would be the Rock on which His Church would be built. How can that possibly happen after everything I've done wrong? *(Pause)* Is there that much forgiveness in Him, even after His death? *(Pause)* And if He can forgive me, what else is possible through Him? Just now, I am so lost that I don't know what to do or where to go . . . so I sit here, in darkness, thinking . . . and the thinking makes it worse. Where is this Man who spoke at length on so many things concerning God and His Kingdom, and who performed so many miraculous acts in His name that it would not be possible to list them all? *(Pause)* His body lies in a cold tomb, sealed and guarded . . . but is that the end of it? I know what was foretold in the Scriptures. We also know what He told us. *(Pause)* Is it true? *(Beat)* Was any of it real? Or was it all a lie? And what if . . . ? *(Long pause)* My heart knows the answer. Even through death, the warmth that pierced my heart so long ago still remains alive, and that's why I'll seek out my brothers at daybreak. *(Turns off light. All performers exit in darkness.)*

Night of Sorrow

by Jill Libramento

A Reader's Theatre piece with two mobile characters

Cast:

NARRATOR
JOANNA
MARY MAGDALENE
PETER
JOHN
ANDREW
THOMAS
SATAN
ANGEL
JESUS

Scene: This Reader's Theatre piece begins immediately after Jesus' death and follows the disciples through those dark hours into the brightness of the resurrection. It ends at the shore where Jesus pulls Peter back from his despair by helping him see that he really does love Jesus, regardless of what his actions may have said. One thing that makes this piece unique is that the characters of Jesus and Satan are in costume and move freely among the readers.

While this is a familiar story, it is the author's hope that the disciples' humanity; their sadness and doubt will be made very real to the audience. Because only one who has been through the night can truly appreciate the morning.

Props:

Music stands or podiums for readers
Three crosses to be illuminated upstage

SFX ***(optional):***

A nail being driven into wood
Knock at the door
Door opening

Costumes: All cast except Jesus and Satan should be dressed entirely in long sleeved, black outfits. Jesus should wear a white robe; Satan, a medieval jester costume in dark tapestry materials, no bells and no hat.

Music and Dance ***(optional):*** This piece was originally performed with music throughout and a ballet at the resurrection. Those notes will be left in, but they are purely optional.

Set: Readers at their podiums should be scattered around the stage with enough room for Jesus and Satan to walk between them. Three crosses are on the back wall of the stage.

Note: The readers should always face forward and never look directly at Satan or another reader. They should put as much emotion and facial expression as they can into their reading. They should not move away from their podium although they can act with their arms and hands. Only when Jesus comes to them can they look at Him. Satan should move slowly and slyly around the readers. He should move in close to them, look at them, whisper in their ears. Jesus should move among the readers and he is allowed to touch them.

Scripture: Scripture is quoted from *Today's English Version* (TEV). Copyright by American Bible Society, 1966, 1971, 1976, 1992. Used by permission.

Running time: Without optional music, approximately 30 minutes; with optional music, approximately 55 minutes

(Actors take their positions in the dark. SFX: Nail being driving into wood as three crosses are illuminated at back of stage. Optional music plays as lights come up and NARRATOR *begins.)*

NARRATOR: "It was about twelve o'clock when the sun stopped shining and darkness covered the whole country until three o'clock. The curtain in the Temple was torn in two from top to bottom. Jesus cried out in a loud voice, 'Father! Into your hands I place my spirit!' He said this and died. The army officer saw what had happened and he praised God saying, 'Certainly He was the Son of God!' When the people who had gathered there to watch the spectacle saw what happened, they all went back home beating their breasts in sorrow." Among them was Mary Magdalene . . .

(Music fades. SATAN *slowly strolls over to* MARY, *circling her as he speaks.)*

SATAN: When I am dead
Think no more of me.
When I am cold,
And my eyes no longer see,
Forgive and forget,
And I will cease to be.
Mary of Magdala, are you sad? Forget. It is over. There is no more.

MARY: I know that voice. I remember you, before Jesus drove you away. Leave me alone!

SATAN: Leave you? Like He did? Then you will truly be alone.

MARY: He said He would not leave us alone.

SATAN: Is He here?

MARY: I am afraid.

SATAN: Of course you are. He built up your hopes, your dreams and for what? For this? *(Points to crosses)* To hang dead on a cross? Ha!

MARY: But this can't be the end!

*(*JOHN *begins his lines;* SATAN *slowly moves away from* MARY *into the shadows.)*

JOHN: Mary? Are you all right? Come on, let's go home. Peter, Thomas, and Joanna are there.

MARY: But what about His body? We can't just leave Him here. He has no grave, we don't have enough money. We weren't expecting this.

JOHN: Joseph of Arimathea has gotten permission to take His body and he is making arrangements to bury it.

MARY: Then Joanna and I must prepare the spices for the burial. I want to go see where the tomb is.

NARRATOR: "Then they went back home and prepared the spices and perfumes for the body. On the Sabbath they rested as the Law commanded."

JOANNA: Mary, are you all right? Come in and rest. I was worried about you.

THOMAS: John, did anyone follow you?

JOHN: I don't think so, but I'll bolt the door. Just to be safe.

THOMAS: You know we must be careful. They have killed Jesus, and they may try to kill us.

JOANNA: Stop talking like that, you two! Aren't things bad enough without borrowing trouble?

THOMAS: I just think we should be careful.

JOHN: I agree with you, Thomas. That's why I took Jesus' mother to my house. She is resting there with Anna.

MARY: John, do you really think she is safe there?

JOHN: I don't know, but I told James to contact me here if anything should happen.

MARY: I think Mary should be here with us.

JOANNA: What about Philip and Matthew?

JOHN: They were going to find Simon and tell him to come here.

THOMAS: OK, then Andrew is on his way and Peter is here . . .

JOANNA *(in a slight whisper):* Yes, Peter. I'm concerned about him. He's not doing well. Thomas, maybe you could talk to him.

(Pause)

THOMAS: Peter. Peter, I know it's hard. It's hard for all of us. I understand.

PETER *(snapping back in anger):* You can't possibly understand! You didn't . . . in the courtyard when they asked me if I knew Him, I . . . I . . .

THOMAS: You what? What happened, Peter?

PETER: The worst thing is that He knew I would do it. He told me I would do it.

THOMAS: Do what, Peter? Tell me.

PETER: And now He's gone. I can't make it right.

THOMAS: What are you talking about, Peter? Make what right?

PETER: Leave me alone, Thomas.

THOMAS: Maybe if you would just talk about it, tell someone . . .

PETER: I said, leave me alone!

JOHN: Thomas, maybe it's best to leave him alone. Andrew will be here soon. He can talk to him.

THOMAS: OK, but John, we really should decide what to do. The authorities will be looking for us. They will want to put an end to Jesus' teachings. They will be trying to get everything back to normal.

MARY: Normal? Normal! What is normal? It's so different now. Everything's changed.

THOMAS: I don't know. I feel so lost. I don't know where to turn. What do we do now?

PETER: Who knows, Thomas? Who cares? It's over! That's all, it's over!

JOHN: What's over, Peter?

PETER: Everything, John! Jesus is dead! We're finished!

JOHN: Finished with what? What were we doing, Peter, that we're now finished? What is over? Were we building a building and now it's finished? Were we preparing a meal and now we've finished eating and we've left the table? What's over?

PETER: You just don't know when to let it go, John. Can't you get it through your head? Jesus is dead! He's gone. We're finished!

SATAN *(moving close to* JOHN*):* Reeling in men with a promise of life,
A promise of love and more.
But it was all too small,
It's dead and gone.
Throw it back in and head for shore.

JOHN: No! I don't know about you, but I loved a Man. I loved Jesus and I haven't stopped loving Him. Death can't stop that. The person that He was changed me. It became part of me and He will go on living through me.

(SATAN moves back into shadows and out of sight during JOHN'S lines. Optional song may be inserted here.)

MARY: I just can't believe Jesus is gone.

JOANNA: I know. This doesn't seem real. It feels like a dream.

THOMAS: Even when we ate with Him last Passover, He said things and you could tell that it was the last time we would all be together. But I just didn't believe it. I just can't believe it.

JOANNA: I can't believe it either. I can still see His face. His laughing face. And His smile.

MARY: And His eyes, those eyes that knew everything.

THOMAS: I just expect Him to come walking through that door any minute.

(SFX: Knock on door, actors are startled.)

THOMAS *(afraid):* Who's there?

ANDREW: It's me, Andrew.

THOMAS: Come in. Come in. Did anyone follow you?

ANDREW: No, I don't think so.

JOHN: Did Philip and Matthew find Simon?

ANDREW: Yes, they're on their way. I didn't stay with them. I went to see Thaddeus, my friend at the Temple.

THOMAS: That was dangerous.

JOHN: What did he say?

ANDREW: He said there was some talk about rounding up Jesus' followers. But nothing yet from the people who would actually give the orders.

JOANNA: Did you see my husband?

ANDREW: Yes, he's on his way and I told some of the others to meet us here. Is everyone here all right?

JOHN: As well as could be expected. Peter is having a tough time of it.

JOANNA: Maybe you should talk to him, Andrew.

ANDREW: I don't think there's anything anyone could say that could make him feel better considering what happened at the courtyard.

(SATAN slinks over to PETER.)

SATAN: Death is as hard as a rock,
And as cold as ice.
But harder and colder still,
When friends deny thee thrice.

(PETER *moans.)*

SATAN: Is it hard, Peter?

PETER: Yes.

SATAN: Is it cold?

PETER: Yes.

SATAN: As hard and cold as death?

PETER: Yes. I wish I could die.

SATAN: And maybe you should. Loving Him, pledging your allegiance to Him and then denying that you even knew Him. Not once . . .

(PETER *moans.)*

SATAN: Not twice . . .

(PETER *moans a little more loudly.)*

SATAN: But three times?

PETER *(in anguish):* Oh! I wish I could die.

(SATAN *slips away into the shadows during* PETER'S *last line. Optional song inserted here.)*

JOHN: It's almost morning and we've been up all night. We all need some rest.

MARY: Rest if you want to, but I'm taking the spices to Jesus.

THOMAS: It's not even light yet. Can't you wait?

MARY: No! This can't wait.

THOMAS: You shouldn't go alone. It's too dangerous.

JOHN: Now, Thomas, let's not get all excited. She can go to the tomb. No one will bother her.

ANDREW: You haven't been out there, John. They may be looking for us right now. Mary, I don't think you should go.

MARY: I'm going to the tomb! Jesus will have a proper burial. That's the least I can do. Joanna, do you want to go with me?

JOANNA: Of course I do.

THOMAS: But I just don't think it's safe!

JOANNA: Don't you understand? We have to go! Jesus needs us now. He's all alone . . . *(begins crying softly)*

SATAN: Death has won!
It was easier than I thought,
To put an end to the lies that He wrought.
I am the victor! The king of it now!
I am the winner! Everyone must bow.

(Optional music plays as NARRATOR *speaks.)*

NARRATOR: "As Sunday morning was dawning, suddenly there was a violent earthquake. An angel of the Lord came down from heaven, rolled the stone away and sat on it. His appearance was like lightning and his clothes were white as snow."

ANGEL: Why do you look for the living among the dead? He is not here. He has risen!

(Optional song and ballet inserted here.)

ANGEL: "Remember how He told you while He was in Galilee: 'The Son of Man must be handed over to sinful men, be crucified and three days later rise to life'?"

NARRATOR: Joanna returned from the tomb and told all these things to the disciples. But Mary stood outside the tomb crying.

JESUS: "Woman. Why are you crying? Who is it you are looking for?"

MARY: Sir, if you have carried Him away, tell me where you have put Him and I will get Him.

JESUS: "Mary."

MARY *(recognizing Him by the way He said her name):* "Rabboni!"

JESUS: "Do not hold on to me, because I have not yet gone back up to the Father. But go to my brothers and tell them that I am returning to him who is my Father and their Father, my God and their God."

NARRATOR: Mary went to where "the disciples were gathered together behind locked doors because they were afraid of the Jewish authorities."

JOHN: Mary! Where have you been? Are you all right?

THOMAS: Andrew, lock the door.

JOANNA: Mary, tell them. You saw the angel too. They won't believe me!

MARY: I have seen the Lord.

JOHN: You have seen . . . Jesus?

JOANNA: We saw an angel, Mary. It wasn't Jesus.

MARY: No, after you left, Joanna. I saw Him—Jesus. He spoke to me.

PETER *(trying to hide his desperation):* What did He say?

ANDREW: Are you sure it was Jesus and not an angel?

JOANNA *(remembering):* His body was not in the tomb.

ANDREW: They probably just took His body away, to another place.

JOHN: But they saw the angel, Andrew. And now Mary says she saw Jesus. Mary wouldn't lie about that. Mary . . . you saw Him?

MARY: Yes.

(They pause in awe and wonder. THOMAS *interrupts.)*

THOMAS: You see this, you see that! I tell you, "unless I see the scars of the nails in His hands and put my finger on those scars and my hand in His side, I will not believe!"

JESUS *(suddenly there):* "Peace be with you."

MARY: Jesus!

ALL: Jesus!

JESUS *(walking to* THOMAS, *facing each other):* "Thomas, put your finger here." See my hands, Thomas? "Reach out your hand and put it in my side. Stop your doubting and believe."

THOMAS *(falling to his knees):* "My Lord and my God!"

JESUS: "Do you believe because you see me? *(Turning to speak to audience)* How happy are those who believe without seeing me!"

(Optional song. All exit stage except PETER, ANDREW, *and* JOHN.*)*

NARRATOR: A few days later, Simon Peter and some others went fishing "but all that night they did not catch a thing. As the sun was rising, Jesus stood at the water's edge, but the disciples did not know it was Jesus."

JESUS *(stepping unto US light and calling out):* "Young men! Haven't you caught anything?"

PETER: "Not a thing!"

JESUS: "Throw your net out on the right side of the boat and you will catch some."

PETER: Are you such a great fisherman that you can see the fish from the shore?

ANDREW *(a little embarrassed by* PETER'S *belligerence):* Just do as He says, Peter. We can't do any worse.

JOHN: Peter! Andrew! Look! The nets are full!

ANDREW: How did that Man know? Only someone like Jesus would know . . .

JOHN: "It is the Lord!"

PETER *(in hopeful awe):* Jesus?

JESUS: "Bring some of the fish you have caught." I've made a fire. Come. Let's eat together.

*(*ANDREW *and* JOHN *quietly exit as* JESUS *goes slowly DS to* PETER.*)*

JESUS: "Simon, son of John, do you love me more than these others do?"

PETER *(pain of his denial on his mind, answers but doesn't look at* JESUS*):* Yes.

JESUS: "Take care of my lambs." *(Uncomfortable pause)* "Simon, son of John, do you love me?"

PETER *(looking at* JESUS, *desperately):* "Yes, Lord, you know that I love you!"

JESUS: "Take care of my sheep." *(Pause)* "Simon, son of John, do you love me?"

Peter *(somewhat agitated):* "Lord, you know everything; you know that I love you!"

(Looking into each others eyes, PETER *realizes that* JESUS *does know all things and knew that* PETER *needed to declare his love for* JESUS *three times to cancel out his three denials.* PETER *grabs* JESUS *and hugs him.)*

JESUS: Take care of my sheep.

*(*JESUS *moves* PETER *away by the shoulders, looking at him intently.)*

JESUS: Follow me.

*(*JESUS *turns and faces audience.* PETER *slips offstage as* JESUS *directs the next lines directly to audience.)*

JESUS: "Go throughout the whole world and preach the gospel to all mankind. Whoever believes and is baptized will be saved; whoever does not believe will be condemned. Believers will be given the power to perform miracles; they will drive out demons in my name; they will speak in strange tongues; if they pick up snakes or drink any poison, they will not be harmed; they will place their hands on sick people, and these will get well.

"Go then to all peoples everywhere and make them my disciples: baptize them in the name of the Father, the Son and the Holy Spirit, and teach them to obey everything I have commanded you. And I will be with you always, even to the end of the age."

(Blackout)